3 200283 624

GW00372490

Transport Statistics Report

Cars : Make and Model : The Risk of Driver Injury and Car Accident Rates in Great Britain : 1992

May 1994

London: HMSO

© Crown Copyright 1994
First published 1994
ISBN 0 11 551267 5

Prepared for publication by STD5 Branch
Directorate of Statistics
Department of Transport

Anthony Craggs
Peter Wilding

GOVERNMENT STATISTICAL SERVICE

A service of statistical information and advice is provided to the government by specialist staff employed in the statistics divisions of individual Departments. Statistics are made generally available through their publications and further information and advice on them can be obtained from the Departments concerned.

Enquiries about the contents of this publication should be made to:

Directorate of Statistics
Department of Transport
Room B649
Romney House
43 Marsham Street
London SW1P 3PY

Telephone 071-276-8780

Contents   Page

INTRODUCTION

This publication presents estimates of the risk of driver injury in popular models of car once involved in a two car collision injury accident. The estimates provide the basis for the calculation of car safety ratings published by the Department in a companion booklet on car safety and security. It also includes, at a more general level, estimates of accident involvement rates and associated casualty rates analysed, within broad groups, by age and performance of car, and whether the car is privately or company owned. The statistics in this publication are based on personal injury road accident data reported to the Department of Transport by police forces within Great Britain. The publication is in two parts.

The first part relates to the risk of driver injury in popular models of car once involved in two car collision injury accidents, generally known as secondary or passive safety. The estimates are shown in Tables A and B. The second part relates to car accident involvement and casualty rates, generally known as primary or active safety, and estimates are shown in Tables C and D.

Structural design is the key factor in secondary safety and is complemented by good design of interior fittings, particularly seat belts, energy absorbing steering wheels and columns, padded dashboards and the provision of airbag supplementary restraints. Together these have great potential for reducing the number of road casualties. By contrast, primary safety - accident avoidance - is mainly influenced by the driver but vehicle design features such as good braking, handling, stability, lighting and driver vision, can all help the driver to avoid accidents.

The first part of the publication summarises the adopted methodology which uses the risk of driver injury as a basis for assessing the secondary safety features of cars, sets out the results in Tables A and B, summarises the main conclusions, and points to future developments. The second part of the publication summarises the accident involvement and casualty rates for particular groups of car, sets out results in Tables C and D, and summarises the main conclusions. This is followed by a section in the form of appendices which set out definitions, and a more detailed description of the source and coverage of the car accident data used in this report for the estimation of car driver injury accident rates.

PART 1

SECONDARY CAR SAFETY (Tables A and B)

Measuring Secondary Car Safety

One approach for assessing secondary car safety is to simulate typical accidents by crashing a car into a fixed block under controlled conditions and, in some cases, to measure the forces on dummy occupants. Such crash tests are able to control the severity of accident and assess the secondary safety design effects in a simulated collision. The shortcoming of these types of test is that they are representative of only some real life collisions.

Another approach to measuring secondary safety is to look at real life injury accident data. This is a more complicated approach because, unlike crash tests where severity of accident can be controlled, severity of real-life accidents can be highly variable which makes it difficult to compare injury data for different car models. This is because different car models may be exposed to different types of accident and may be driven predominantly by different groups of drivers.

The measure of secondary safety for popular models of cars in this publication is based upon the risk of driver injury in two car collisions. This is a relatively straightforward calculation because in every injury accident it is known whether the driver is injured or uninjured because every car must have a driver, except for parked cars which are not included in the analysis. A fuller measure of secondary car safety could also include the risk of injury to front seat passengers. However this is not so straightforward to calculate because only information on injured passengers is recorded by the police, and any risk calculation would have to be based on assumptions about the average number of front seat passengers in models of car to which the number of injured front seat passengers could be compared. Since average front seat occupancy is likely to be variable in different models of car, it was decided to measure secondary safety on the narrower but more reliable definition of driver injury only.

In this section, for any injury accident involving a particular model of car, the risk of driver injury is expressed as the proportion of injury accidents in which drivers of that model are injured. These proportions, or rates, are relative rates in the sense that in any two car collision, the relative risk of driver injury not only depends upon the protection offered by the car being driven but also the safety performance of the car being hit. Most popular models of car tend to collide with a similar range of other cars in two car collisions, so for each model the risk of driver injury in that model is being assessed relative to the same average level of safety offered by injury accident involved cars.

An interesting point to note is the influence of interior, as distinct from exterior, secondary safety features upon the risk of injury in, say, two car collisions. If only one of the cars in a two car collision is fitted with an interior secondary safety device (such as an airbag) then the relative risk of driver injury in that car will be lower. If one of the cars in a two car collision is fitted with better exterior safety devices (such as superior energy absorbing bumpers or crumple zones) the relative risk of injury to both drivers in that particular collision is not affected, since the benefit of these devices is shared equally by both cars. However over the whole range of accidents the beneficial effects upon the risk of driver injury will be relatively concentrated on those models fitted with a superior exterior secondary safety device.

In general, mass and size of car are closely related. However in larger cars there is usually more room for crumple zones which absorb energy and reduce deceleration forces upon the driver and occupants, reducing their risk of injury. The benefits of size and mass are not available to the same extent in smaller cars. However, mass is a double edged sword to the extent that a heavier car will increase the risk of injury to the driver in the other car involved in the collision.

In this publication, the risk of driver injury in an injury accident provides the basis for assessing the protection that a car offers its driver. The main methodological problem in comparing driver injury risk in different cars is that the risks are influenced not only by the cars' safety features, but also by the severity of each of the individual accidents in which they are involved. The average severity of accident for each model will be influenced not only by the types of accident they are involved in, but also by the type of driver group which predominates in a particular model of car. For example, some cars may be involved in relatively more injury accidents on motorways at higher speeds than other cars, and some may be driven more by women whose risk of injury once involved in an accident is higher than that for men. A recent study by Dr Jeremy Broughton at the Transport Research Laboratory "The theoretical basis for comparing the accident record of car models" (see References in Appendix 1) showed the broad extent to which different models of car are driven by different groups of driver and are involved in accidents on built-up and non built-up roads.

Only accidents involving two car collisions are considered in the assessment of car secondary safety in order to minimise distortions to the estimates of driver injury risk arising, for example, from a particular model of car having a high proportion of collisions with very large mass vehicles like heavy goods vehicles or coaches. Within the two car accident dataset there will still be some bias in the estimates of driver injury risk for each car model because of the different types of accident and driver involvement for some models of car. These influences are allowed for in a modelling procedure described in Appendix 5. In fact the adjustments made to estimates of driver injury risk to allow for these sources of bias are quite small. Nevertheless the adjusted estimates are the best estimates of secondary car safety derived from the two car collision dataset, and reflect the benefit of the secondary safety protection offered to the driver of a particular car, as well as the benefit of the size or mass of that car.

In addition to speed a major influence on the severity of accident is the mass of the car. In any two car collision the greater the mass of one of the cars involved in the collision the lower the deceleration force and risk of driver injury in that car. However in that same collision the deceleration force and risk of driver injury in the other lower mass car will usually be higher. Although mass provides safety benefits for the driver of a high mass car it also increases the risk of driver injury in those cars in collision with high mass cars.

Most models of car collide with a similar size distribution of other cars involved in the collision. Appendix 4 shows the distribution of collisions for each model in relation to the broad size group of the other car involved in the collision. At this broad level of aggregation the distributions are very similar. This leads to the conclusion that in two car accidents a safety rating for each model is calculated as if each car had collided with a car of average mass. But if finer dissagregation of the

From an individual driver's point of view the mass of car is certainly to be regarded as a safety factor, because the laws of physics determine that they will be safer in most accidents when they are driving a heavier or larger car. However it would be interesting to compare cars only on the basis of the secondary protection that is offered by their structure, design and secondary safety fittings. This requires a procedure to remove the influence of mass from the calculation of risk of driver injury. Once the appropriate mass data have been assimilated, we expect to be able to remove the specific effects of mass from the relative risks of driver injury so that relative safety assessments of car models can be made in terms of their inherent design features and secondary safety fittings. In Table A, and the Department's accompanying booklet on car safety and security, cars have been classified into four size groups. Within each of the size groups the variation in mass between cars will be less than the variation in mass between cars in different size groups. This means that the risk of driver injury in cars of broadly similar mass within each size group can be compared to assess the protection offered by the structure and design of the car and its secondary safety fittings. But even within the four size groups there remains some mass variation.

Table A : Description

Table A sets out estimates of the risk of driver injury in all two car driver injury accidents, for particular models of car, in four size groups, broadly defined by length of car. The estimates are based on accidents involving two cars during the years 1989, 1990, 1991 and 1992. Ratings are only published for cars first registered on or after 1st January 1983. The rating for all sizes of car includes those models for which results are not presented individually while the size group averages are based on a weighted average of those models listed in the respective group. The calculation of the risk as the percentage of drivers injured in a specific model of car (say car 1) when involved in an injury accident with any other car (say car 2) can be represented schematically as follows:

$$\frac{X_1 + X_2}{X_1 + X_2 + X_3} \times 100$$

where

X_1 = Number of accidents in which driver injured in car 1 but not in car 2
X_2 = Number of accidents in which driver injured in car 1 and in car 2
X_3 = Number of accidents in which driver injured in car 2 but not in car 1

Within each size group (Small, Small/Medium, Medium, and Large) estimates are shown for each constituent model of car for all injuries and for fatal or serious injuries. The confidence intervals are also shown for each estimate for each car model. These show the range within which 95 per cent of the time the estimate will lie. For both fatal or serious injuries and all injuries, uncorrected estimates (where no allowances have been made for types of accident or types of driver on the injury rates) are shown in brackets. The corrected estimates are shown (not in brackets) alongside their respective confidence intervals. It can be seen that allowing for variation in the type of accidents and type of driver in specific car models does not have a great effect. However some of the allowances are only based on approximate indicators (speed of road as an indicator for speed of accident) and it may be that the available data are not sensitive enough to pick up such effects. The estimates in Table A are based only on two car accidents, which has the benefit of directly eliminating the possibly distorting effects on the ratings, for some models of car, of a higher incidence of single vehicle accidents and collisions with large mass vehicles such as Goods Vehicles and Public Service Vehicles.

The most significant adjustment was for female drivers. Female drivers are more prone to injury for a given severity of accident and they tend to drive smaller cars than men. The main adjustment therefore tended to improve the uncorrected ratings for small cars where there was a higher incidence of women drivers, but to degrade the uncorrected ratings for large cars where there was a lower incidence of female drivers. Details of the adjustment process for driver influence and type of accident which influence severity of accident can be found in Appendix 5.

Table A : Commentary

The corrected best estimates of the percentage of drivers injured in any particular model, and their associated confidence intervals, can be used to assess which cars in any group are significantly different from the average risk for the group. Those models with a higher than average risk of driver injury offer a lower than average level of secondary protection, and vice versa for those models with a lower than average risk of driver injury. The estimates have been calculated after allowances have been made for the possible influence of exposure to different types of accident and driver. The specific influences that were looked at were age and sex of driver, point of impact, and speed limit of road as an indicator of severity of accident. More models are identified as being statistically different from their relevant group average for all injuries than for fatal or serious injuries because of the much larger proportions in the samples for all injuries compared to fatal or serious injuries. Consequently the confidence intervals are narrower for all injuries (see Appendix 3).

Particular car models can be said to be statistically different (95 per cent of the time) from their respective group average if that average lies outside the confidence interval for the particular model. For example, in the grouping of small size cars shown in Table A the Citroen 2CV/Dyane is statistically different from the average risk of driver injury (for all injuries) in all small cars since the confidence interval for the Citroen model (79 to 88 per cent) does not include the estimate of average risk in all small cars (71 per cent). Similarly differences between particular models can be identified if the respective confidence intervals do not overlap. For example, the confidence interval for the Citroen 2CV/Dyane (79 to 88 per cent) does not overlap with the confidence interval for the Renault 5 Jan 83 to Jan 85 (55 to 67 per cent).

The four groups of car shown in Table A have been determined by length of car. Within each of the groups the specific model groupings of car have been determined by considering production line information about specific car models to ensure that the model groupings consist of models with as uniform design as possible. There will be some variation in mass between car models in each of the size groups despite the attempt to standardize the size classification of the four car groups. The estimates of risk of injury for each car model within each size group will reflect variations in mass, and also the secondary safety design and fittings features offered by each model, and current work is focusing on how to allow for the influence of mass in car collisions so that the risk of injury estimates mainly reflect the influence of structural design and safety fittings in cars. The important effect of mass and size on risk of injury is clearly shown in Table A. The group average of 71 per cent for small cars falls steadily with group size to 45 per cent for large cars, confirming that, generally, the greater the mass of the car the greater the safety benefit to the driver of that car involved in a collision. In addition, drivers of larger cars are more likely to benefit from more extensive crumple zones. However, it is also true that the greater the risk of injury in the car that it collides with. This a~~ current investigation, and it is planned in the fut~~ reflect the protective benefit of mass, the~ structural design and safety f~~~

The est~~ safety ratings for car models published in ~ four graphs following the commentary on Table ~. within each of the four size groups. The safety rating is ~~

Table A and relates the risk of injury in a particular model of car to the risk of injury in the overall average car. For example the rating for the Volvo 300 (small/medium cars) is calculated as follows:

All Injury risk (Volvo 300) best estimate   =   54%

All Injury risk (Overall Average car) best estimate =   63%

$$\text{Safety Rating} = \frac{63\% - 54\%}{63\%} \times 100 = +13\%$$

This shows that the safety rating for the Volvo 300, in terms of the statistical best estimate, is 13 per cent more than that for the overall average car. A similar calculation is carried out to show how the confidence interval for the safety rating, which includes the best estimate, relates to the overall average car, and these confidence intervals are shown in the four graphs. For example the confidence interval for the Volvo 300 shows that the estimate of the safety rating for this car could be between 9 and 17 per cent better than for the overall average car. The graphs show the confidence interval for each model's rating. Although the ratings have been calculated with reference to the overall average car, the graphs show them in relation to both the overall average and also their respective group average. Within each group of similar sized cars the graphs clearly show groups of cars which, at the 95 per cent level of confidence, are statistically different from their group average, and also from other models within the same group. The following table shows the distribution of these differences within each size group:

Car Size	Below Group Average	Around Group Average	Above Group Average	All Models
Small	3	14	2	19
Small/medium	6	20	8	34
Medium	3	17	9	29
Large	5	9	5	19
All	17	60	24	101

In each graph, make/models are presented alphabetically within the following three groups; models whose confidence intervals fall entirely below, around and entirely above the average for that size group. The effect of size and mass upon the ratings shows through when the confidence intervals are compared with the overall average. The intervals for small cars mostly fall below the overall average line, but the intervals for large cars all fall above the overall average line.

Relative driver protection by make/model 1989-92
Small cars

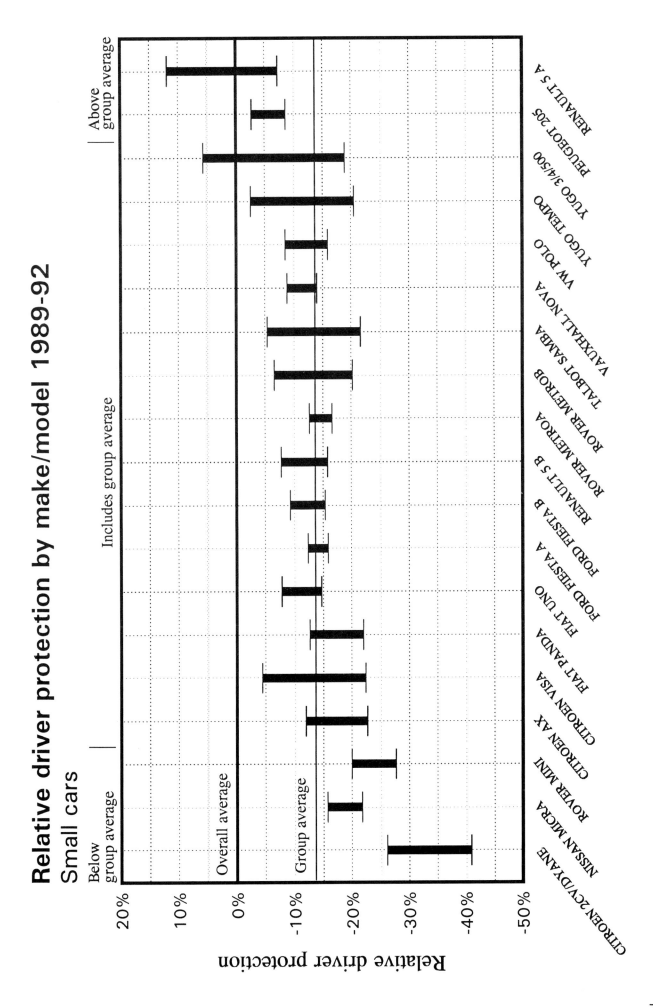

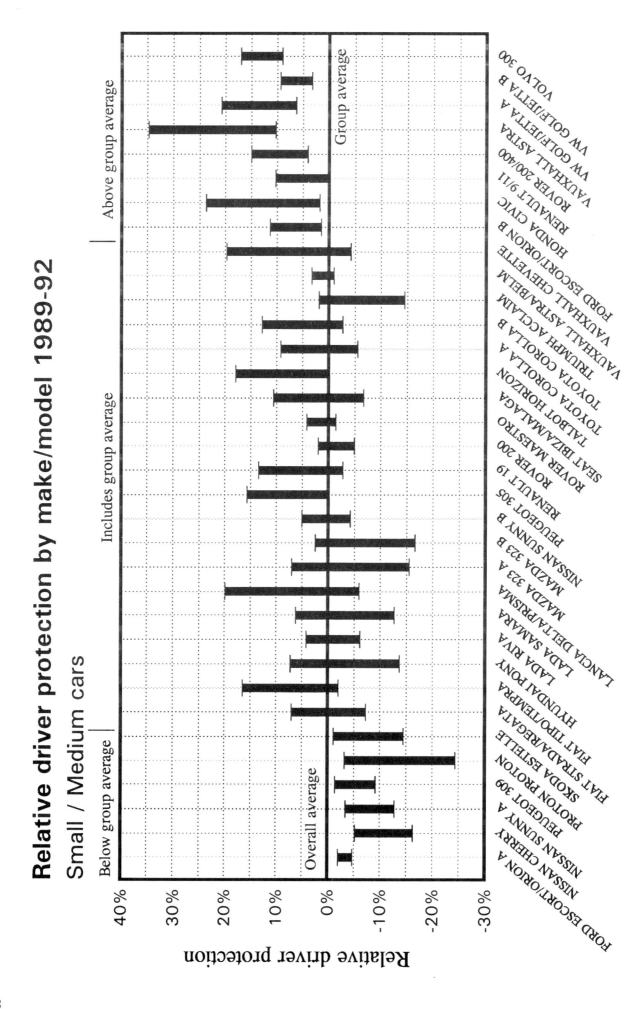

Relative driver protection by make/model 1989-92

Small / Medium cars

Relative driver protection

40% 30% 20% 10% 0% -10% -20% -30%

Below group average
Includes group average
Above group average

Overall average
Group average

FORD ESCORT/ORION A
NISSAN CHERRY
NISSAN SUNNY A
PEUGEOT 309
PROTON
SKODA ESTELLE
FIAT STRADA/REGATA
FIAT TIPO/TEMPRA
HYUNDAI PONY
LADA RIVA
LADA SAMARA
LANCIA DELTA/PRISMA
MAZDA 323 A
MAZDA 323 B
NISSAN SUNNY B
PEUGEOT 305
RENAULT 19
ROVER 200
SEAT IBIZA/MALAGA
TALBOT HORIZON
TOYOTA COROLLA B
TOYOTA COROLLA A
TRIUMPH ACCLAIM
VAUXHALL ASTRA/BELM
FORD ESCORT/ORION B
HONDA CIVIC
RENAULT 9/11
ROVER 200/400
VAUXHALL ASTRA
VW GOLF/JETTA A
VW GOLF/JETTA B
VOLVO 300

8

Relative driver protection by make/model 1989-92

Medium cars

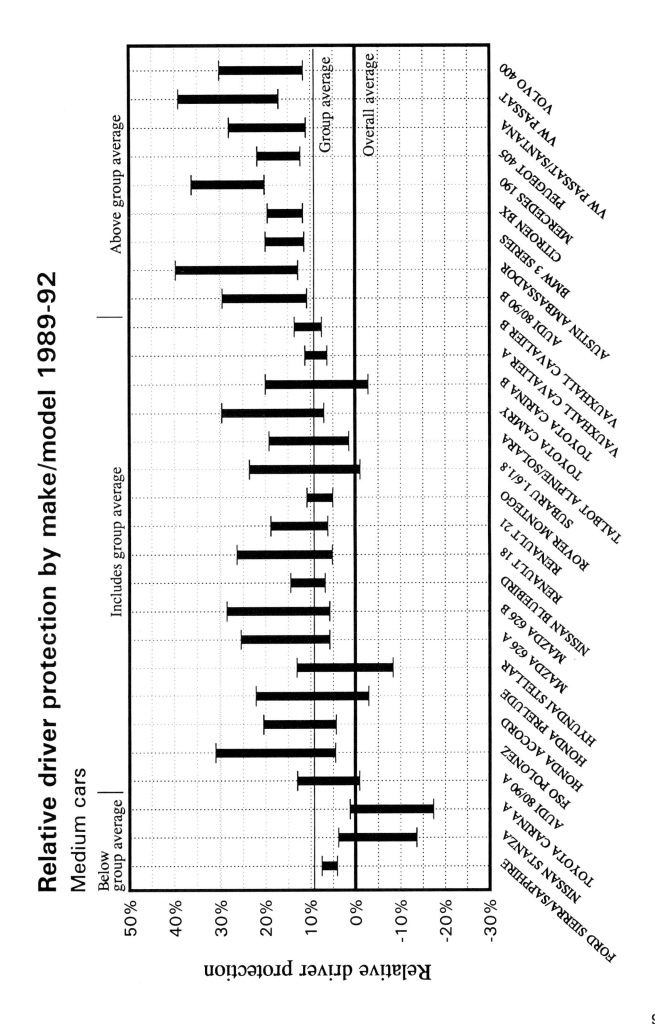

Relative driver protection by make/model 1989-92

Large cars

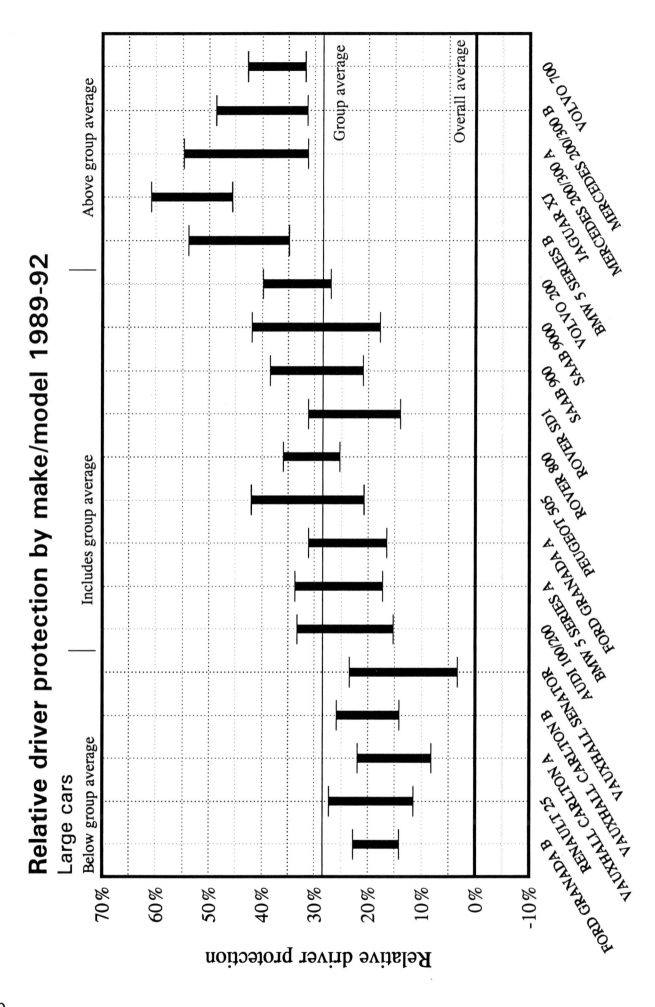

GUIDE TO MAKE/MODELS IN GRAPHS

Car size/model	Registration dates	Car size/model	Registration dates
SMALL		**SMALL/MEDIUM**	
CITROEN 2CV/DYANE	Jan 83 - Jul 90	FIAT STRADA/REGATA	Jan 83 - Jun 88
CITROEN AX	Jun 87 - Dec 92	FIAT TIPO/TEMPRA	Jul 88 - Dec 92
CITROEN VISA	Jan 83 - Jul 88	FORD ESCORT/ORION A	Jan 83 - Aug 90
FIAT PANDA	Jan 83 - Dec 92	FORD ESCORT/ORION B	Sep 90 - Dec 92
FIAT UNO	Jun 83 - Dec 92	HONDA CIVIC	Oct 87 - Oct 91
FORD FIESTA A	Jan 83 - Mar 89	HYUNDAI PONY	Oct 85 - Aug 90
FORD FIESTA B	Apr 89 - Dec 92	LADA RIVA	Jan 83 - Dec 92
NISSAN MICRA	Jun 83 - Dec 92	LADA SAMARA	Nov 87 - Dec 92
PEUGEOT 205	Oct 83 - Dec 92	LANCIA DELTA/PRISMA	Jan 83 - Dec 92
RENAULT 5 A	Jan 83 - Jan 85	MAZDA 323 A	Jan 83 - Aug 85
RENAULT 5 B	Feb 85 - Dec 92	MAZDA 323 B	Sep 85 - Sep 89
ROVER METRO A	Jan 83 - Mar 90	NISSAN CHERRY	Jan 83 - Aug 86
ROVER METRO B	Apr 90 - Dec 92	NISSAN SUNNY A	Jan 83 - Aug 86
ROVER MINI	Jan 83 - Dec 92	NISSAN SUNNY B	Sep 86 - Jan 91
TALBOT SAMBA	Jan 83 - Sep 86	PEUGEOT 305	Jan 83 - Jul 88
VAUXHALL NOVA	Apr 83 - Dec 92	PEUGEOT 309	Feb 86 - Dec 92
VOLKSWAGEN POLO	Jan 83 - Dec 92	PROTON PROTON	Mar 89 - Dec 92
YUGO 3/4/500	Jan 83 - Dec 91	RENAULT 19	Feb 89 - Dec 92
YUGO TEMPO	May 83 - Dec 92	RENAULT 9/11	Jan 83 - Jan 89
		ROVER 200	Jun 84 - Sep 89
		ROVER 200/400	Oct 89 - Dec 92
		ROVER MAESTRO	Mar 83 - Dec 92
		SEAT IBIZA/MALAGA	Oct 85 - Dec 92
		SKODA ESTELLE	Jan 83 - Jul 90
		TALBOT HORIZON	Jan 83 - Dec 85
		TOYOTA COROLLA A	Sep 83 - Aug 87
		TOYOTA COROLLA B	Sep 87 - Jul 92
MEDIUM		TRIUMPH ACCLAIM	Jan 83 - May 84
AUDI 80/90 A	Jan 83 - Oct 86	VAUXHALL ASTRA/BELMONT	Oct 84 - Sep 91
AUDI 80/90 B	Nov 86 - Dec 92	VAUXHALL ASTRA	Oct 91 - Dec 92
AUSTIN AMBASSADOR	Jan 83 - Jan 84	VAUXHALL CHEVETTE	Jan 83 - Aug 84
BMW 3 SERIES	Jan 83 - Mar 91	VOLKSWAGEN GOLF/JETTA A	Jan 83 - Feb 84
CITROEN BX	Aug 83 - Dec 92	VOLKSWAGEN GOLF/JETTA B	Mar 84 - Dec 92
FORD SIERRA/SAPPHIRE	Jan 83 - Dec 92	VOLVO 300	Jan 83 - Dec 91
FSO POLONEZ	Jan 83 - Dec 91		
HONDA ACCORD	Oct 85 - Sep 91		
HONDA PRELUDE	Mar 83 - Mar 92		
HYUNDAI STELLAR	Jun 84 - Dec 92		
MAZDA 626 A	May 83 - Sep 87		
MAZDA 626 B	Oct 87 - Jan 92	**LARGE**	
MERCEDES 190	Sep 83 - Dec 92	AUDI 100/200	Jan 83 - Dec 92
NISSAN BLUEBIRD	Mar 86 - Aug 90	BMW 5 SERIES A	Jan 83 - May 88
NISSAN STANZA	Jan 83 - Dec 86	BMW 5 SERIES B	Jun 88 - Dec 92
PEUGEOT 405	Jan 88 - Dec 92	FORD GRANADA A	Jan 83 - Apr 85
RENAULT 18	Jan 83 - May 86	FORD GRANADA B	May 85 - Dec 92
RENAULT 21	Jun 86 - Dec 92	JAGUAR XJ	Oct 86 - Dec 92
ROVER MONTEGO	Apr 84 - Dec 92	MERCEDES 200/300 A	Jan 83 - Sep 85
SUBARU 1.6/1.8	Nov 84 - Dec 91	MERCEDES 200/300 B	Oct 85 - Dec 92
TALBOT ALPINE/SOLARA	Jan 83 - Dec 86	PEUGEOT 505	Jan 83 - Dec 91
TOYOTA CAMRY	May 83 - Dec 86	RENAULT 25	Jul 84 - Dec 92
TOYOTA CARINA A	Apr 84 - Feb 88	ROVER 800	Jul 86 - Dec 92
TOYOTA CARINA B	Mar 88 - Apr 92	ROVER SD1	Jan 83 - Jun 86
VAUXHALL CAVALIER A	Jan 83 - Sep 88	SAAB 900	Jan 83 - Dec 92
VAUXHALL CAVALIER B	Oct 88 - Dec 92	SAAB 9000	Oct 85 - Dec 92
VOLKSWAGEN PASSAT/SANTANA	Jan 83 - May 88	VAUXHALL CARLTON A	Jan 83 - Oct 86
VOLKSWAGEN PASSAT	Jun 88 - Dec 92	VAUXHALL CARLTON B	Nov 86 - Dec 92
VOLVO 400	Jun 87 - Dec 92	VAUXHALL SENATOR	Sep 87 - Dec 92
		VOLVO 200	Jan 83 - Dec 92
		VOLVO 700	Jan 83 - Jul 91

Table A   Risk of injury to car drivers involved in two car injury accidents: by size and make/model of car: 1989 to 1992

		Percentage of drivers injured when involved in an injury accident[1]					
		Injury severity					
		Fatal or serious			All		
Car size/model[2]	Registration dates	Corrected[3]	95% C.I.[4]	Uncorrected	Corrected[3]	95% C.I.[4]	Uncorrected
SMALL							
CITROEN 2CV/DYANE	Jan 83 - Jul 90[5]	11	[8 , 15]	(11)	84	[79 , 88]	(86)
CITROEN AX	Jun 87 - Dec 92	8	[7 , 11]	(9)	74	[70 , 77]	(76)
CITROEN VISA	Jan 83 - Jul 88[5]	11	[8 , 15]	(12)	71	[65 , 77]	(73)
FIAT PANDA	Jan 83 - Dec 92	9	[7 , 11]	(8)	73	[70 , 76]	(76)
FIAT UNO	Jun 83 - Dec 92	8	[7 , 9]	(8)	70	[67 , 72]	(70)
FORD FIESTA	Jan 83 - Mar 89	9	[8 , 10]	(9)	71	[70 , 72]	(73)
FORD FIESTA	Apr 89 - Dec 92	7	[6 , 9]	(7)	70	[68 , 72]	(71)
NISSAN MICRA	Jun 83 - Dec 92	9	[8 , 10]	(9)	74	[72 , 76]	(77)
PEUGEOT 205	Oct 83 - Dec 92	9	[8 , 10]	(9)	66	[64 , 68]	(68)
RENAULT 5	Jan 83 - Jan 85	7	[5 , 11]	(8)	61	[55 , 67]	(66)
RENAULT 5	Feb 85 - Dec 92	9	[8 , 10]	(9)	70	[67 , 72]	(71)
ROVER METRO	Jan 83 - Mar 90	9	[8 , 9]	(8)	72	[70 , 73]	(75)
ROVER METRO	Apr 90 - Dec 92	8	[6 , 11]	(8)	71	[67 , 75]	(71)
ROVER MINI	Jan 83 - Dec 92	12	[10 , 13]	(11)	78	[75 , 80]	(82)
TALBOT SAMBA	Jan 83 - Sep 86[5]	7	[5 , 10]	(7)	71	[66 , 76]	(76)
VAUXHALL NOVA	Apr 83 - Dec 92	8	[7 , 9]	(8)	70	[68 , 71]	(73)
VOLKSWAGEN POLO	Jan 83 - Dec 92	8	[7 , 10]	(9)	70	[68 , 73]	(73)
YUGO 3/4/500	Jan 83 - Dec 91	12	[8 , 18]	(12)	67	[59 , 74]	(66)
YUGO TEMPO	May 83 - Dec 92	5	[3 , 9]	(5)	70	[64 , 75]	(71)
ALL SMALL		9		(8)	71		(74)
SMALL/MEDIUM							
FIAT STRADA/REGATA	Jan 83 - Jun 88[5]	10	[7 , 13]	(9)	63	[58 , 67]	(59)
FIAT TIPO/TEMPRA	Jul 88 - Dec 92	5	[3 , 8]	(5)	58	[52 , 64]	(55)
FORD ESCORT/ORION	Jan 83 - Aug 90	8	[7 , 8]	(7)	65	[64 , 65]	(62)
FORD ESCORT/ORION	Sep 90 - Dec 92	6	[5 , 7]	(6)	59	[55 , 62]	(55)
HONDA CIVIC	Oct 87 - Oct 91	6	[4 , 10]	(6)	55	[48 , 61]	(60)
HYUNDAI PONY	Oct 85 - Aug 90	11	[7 , 15]	(12)	65	[58 , 71]	(65)
LADA RIVA[6]	Jan 83 - Dec 92	7	[6 , 9]	(8)	63	[60 , 66]	(60)
LADA SAMARA	Nov 87 - Dec 92	5	[3 , 9]	(6)	65	[59 , 70]	(63)
LANCIA DELTA/PRISMA	Jan 83 - Dec 92	11	[7 , 17]	(11)	58	[50 , 66]	(52)
MAZDA 323	Jan 83 - Aug 85	8	[5 , 13]	(8)	66	[58 , 72]	(66)
MAZDA 323	Sep 85 - Sep 89	7	[5 , 11]	(8)	67	[61 , 73]	(68)
NISSAN CHERRY	Jan 83 - Aug 86[5]	10	[8 , 12]	(9)	69	[66 , 73]	(69)
NISSAN SUNNY	Jan 83 - Aug 86	9	[7 , 11]	(8)	68	[65 , 71]	(65)
NISSAN SUNNY	Sep 86 - Jan 91	7	[6 , 9]	(7)	62	[59 , 65]	(61)
PEUGEOT 305	Jan 83 - Jul 88[5]	7	[5 , 9]	(7)	58	[53 , 63]	(54)
PEUGEOT 309	Feb 86 - Dec 92	8	[7 , 10]	(9)	66	[63 , 68]	(65)
PROTON PROTON	Mar 89 - Dec 92	10	[6 , 15]	(10)	72	[65 , 78]	(69)
RENAULT 19	Feb 89 - Dec 92	7	[5 , 10]	(8)	59	[54 , 64]	(58)
RENAULT 9/11	Jan 83 - Jan 89[5]	8	[7 , 10]	(8)	59	[56 , 63]	(60)
ROVER 200	Jun 84 - Sep 89	8	[7 , 9]	(8)	63	[61 , 66]	(62)
ROVER 200/400	Oct 89 - Dec 92	7	[6 , 9]	(8)	57	[53 , 60]	(54)
ROVER MAESTRO	Mar 83 - Dec 92	6	[6 , 7]	(7)	62	[60 , 63]	(60)
SEAT IBIZA/MALAGA	Oct 85 - Dec 92	7	[4 , 10]	(7)	61	[56 , 67]	(62)
SKODA ESTELLE	Jan 83 - Jul 90[5]	9	[7 , 11]	(9)	68	[63 , 72]	(70)
TALBOT HORIZON	Jan 83 - Dec 85[5]	6	[4 , 9]	(6)	57	[51 , 62]	(60)
TOYOTA COROLLA	Sep 83 - Aug 87	9	[7 , 12]	(8)	61	[57 , 66]	(60)
TOYOTA COROLLA	Sep 87 - Jul 92	6	[4 , 9]	(7)	59	[54 , 64]	(61)
TRIUMPH ACCLAIM	Jan 83 - May 84[5]	6	[4 , 9]	(6)	67	[61 , 72]	(67)
VAUXHALL ASTRA/BELMONT	Oct 84 - Sep 91	7	[6 , 8]	(7)	62	[60 , 63]	(59)
VAUXHALL ASTRA	Oct 91 - Dec 92	3	[2 , 7]	(3)	48	[41 , 56]	(48)
VAUXHALL CHEVETTE	Jan 83 - Aug 84[5]	6	[3 , 10]	(6)	58	[50 , 65]	(62)
VOLKSWAGEN GOLF/JETTA	Jan 83 - Feb 84	6	[4 , 8]	(6)	54	[50 , 59]	(52)
VOLKSWAGEN GOLF/JETTA	Mar 84 - Dec 92	7	[6 , 8]	(7)	59	[57 , 60]	(58)
VOLVO 300	Jan 83 - Dec 91[5]	6	[5 , 7]	(6)	54	[52 , 57]	(57)
ALL SMALL/MEDIUM		7		(7)	63		(61)

1   Excluding accidents in which neither driver was injured.
2   Models are listed under the current market name of the manufacturer.
3   Corrected for selected accident circumstances such as road type and driver age. Uncorrected rates are shown in brackets.
4   The probability is 95% that the true rate lies within the range.
5   Approximate withdrawal date. All cars registered up to December 1992 are included.
6   Includes earlier 1200, 1300, 1500 and 1600 models.

Table A (cont'd) Risk of injury to car drivers involved in two car injury accidents: by size and make/model of car: 1989 to 1992

Percentage of drivers injured when involved in an injury accident[1]

Car size/model[2]	Registration dates	Injury severity					
		Fatal or serious			All		
		Corrected[3]	95% C.I.[4]	Uncorrected	Corrected[3]	95% C.I.[4]	Uncorrected
MEDIUM							
AUDI 80/90	Jan 83 - Oct 86	7	[5 , 10]	(7)	59	[54 , 63]	(56)
AUDI 80/90	Nov 86 - Dec 92	4	[2 , 7]	(5)	50	[44 , 56]	(49)
AUSTIN AMBASSADOR	Jan 83 - Jan 84[5]	7	[4 , 13]	(8)	46	[38 , 55]	(41)
BMW 3 SERIES	Jan 83 - Mar 91	7	[5 , 8]	(6)	53	[50 , 55]	(50)
CITROEN BX	Aug 83 - Dec 92	5	[4 , 6]	(6)	53	[50 , 55]	(48)
FORD SIERRA/SAPPHIRE	Jan 83 - Dec 92	7	[6 , 7]	(7)	59	[58 , 60]	(54)
FSO POLONEZ	Jan 83 - Dec 91[5]	6	[3 , 11]	(6)	52	[43 , 60]	(50)
HONDA ACCORD	Oct 85 - Sep 91	8	[6 , 11]	(8)	55	[50 , 60]	(55)
HONDA PRELUDE	Mar 83 - Mar 92	4	[2 , 9]	(5)	57	[49 , 64]	(56)
HYUNDAI STELLAR	Jun 84 - Dec 92	4	[2 , 8]	(4)	61	[54 , 68]	(56)
MAZDA 626	May 83 - Sep 87	5	[3 , 8]	(4)	53	[47 , 59]	(50)
MAZDA 626	Oct 87 - Jan 92	9	[6 , 14]	(10)	52	[45 , 59]	(51)
MERCEDES 190	Sep 83 - Dec 92	5	[3 , 8]	(5)	45	[40 , 50]	(42)
NISSAN BLUEBIRD	Mar 86 - Aug 90[5]	6	[4 , 7]	(5)	56	[54 , 58]	(51)
NISSAN STANZA	Jan 83 - Dec 86[5]	8	[6 , 12]	(7)	66	[60 , 71]	(62)
PEUGEOT 405	Jan 88 - Dec 92	5	[4 , 7]	(6)	52	[49 , 55]	(49)
RENAULT 18	Jan 83 - May 86[5]	7	[4 , 11]	(7)	53	[46 , 59]	(52)
RENAULT 21	Jun 86 - Dec 92	6	[4 , 8]	(6)	55	[51 , 59]	(51)
ROVER MONTEGO	Apr 84 - Dec 92	7	[6 , 8]	(7)	58	[56 , 59]	(53)
SUBARU 1.6/1.8	Nov 84 - Dec 91	5	[3 , 9]	(7)	56	[48 , 63]	(58)
TALBOT ALPINE/SOLARA	Jan 83 - Dec 86[5]	6	[4 , 9]	(7)	56	[51 , 62]	(57)
TOYOTA CAMRY	May 83 - Dec 86	7	[5 , 12]	(8)	51	[44 , 58]	(45)
TOYOTA CARINA	Apr 84 - Feb 88	5	[3 , 9]	(5)	68	[62 , 73]	(64)
TOYOTA CARINA	Mar 88 - Apr 92	8	[5 , 12]	(9)	57	[50 , 64]	(54)
VAUXHALL CAVALIER	Jan 83 - Sep 88	6	[6 , 7]	(6)	57	[56 , 59]	(52)
VAUXHALL CAVALIER	Oct 88 - Dec 92	6	[5 , 6]	(6)	56	[54 , 58]	(51)
VOLKSWAGEN PASSAT/SANTANA	Jan 83 - May 88	6	[4 , 9]	(7)	50	[45 , 56]	(50)
VOLKSWAGEN PASSAT	Jun 88 - Dec 92	5	[3 , 8]	(6)	45	[38 , 52]	(41)
VOLVO 400	Jun 87 - Dec 92	6	[4 , 9]	(7)	50	[44 , 55]	(51)
ALL MEDIUM		6		(6)	57		(52)
LARGE							
AUDI 100/200	Jan 83 - Dec 92	3	[2 , 5]	(4)	47	[42 , 53]	(44)
BMW 5 SERIES	Jan 83 - May 88	4	[3 , 6]	(4)	47	[41 , 52]	(44)
BMW 5 SERIES	Jun 88 - Dec 92	5	[3 , 8]	(4)	35	[29 , 41]	(30)
FORD GRANADA	Jan 83 - Apr 85	5	[3 , 7]	(5)	48	[43 , 52]	(42)
FORD GRANADA	May 85 - Dec 92	6	[5 , 8]	(7)	51	[48 , 54]	(47)
JAGUAR XJ	Oct 86 - Dec 92	3	[2 , 5]	(3)	29	[24 , 34]	(28)
MERCEDES 200/300	Jan 83 - Sep 85	2	[1 , 6]	(2)	35	[28 , 43]	(34)
MERCEDES 200/300	Oct 85 - Dec 92	5	[3 , 8]	(5)	37	[32 , 43]	(36)
PEUGEOT 505	Jan 83 - Dec 91[5]	3	[1 , 5]	(3)	43	[36 , 50]	(41)
RENAULT 25	Jul 84 - Dec 92	6	[4 , 8]	(6)	50	[45 , 55]	(45)
ROVER 800	Jul 86 - Dec 92	4	[3 , 5]	(5)	43	[40 , 47]	(38)
ROVER SD1	Jan 83 - Jun 86[5]	5	[4 , 8]	(5)	48	[43 , 54]	(46)
SAAB 900	Jan 83 - Dec 92	4	[2 , 6]	(5)	44	[39 , 49]	(41)
SAAB 9000	Oct 85 - Dec 92	3	[2 , 6]	(4)	44	[36 , 51]	(42)
VAUXHALL CARLTON	Jan 83 - Oct 86	6	[4 , 8]	(5)	53	[49 , 57]	(49)
VAUXHALL CARLTON	Nov 86 - Dec 92	5	[4 , 6]	(5)	50	[46 , 54]	(45)
VAUXHALL SENATOR	Sep 87 - Dec 92	5	[3 , 8]	(5)	54	[48 , 60]	(48)
VOLVO 200	Jan 83 - Dec 92	5	[3 , 7]	(5)	42	[38 , 46]	(41)
VOLVO 700	Jan 83 - Jul 91[5]	3	[2 , 5]	(4)	39	[36 , 43]	(37)
ALL LARGE		4		(5)	45		(42)
ALL SIZES		8		(7)	63		(61)

1 Excluding accidents in which neither driver was injured.

2 Models are listed under the current market name of the manufacturer.

3 Corrected for selected accident circumstances such as road type and driver age. Uncorrected rates are shown in brackets.

4 The probability is 95% that the true rate lies within the range.

5 Approximate withdrawal date. All cars registered up to December 1992 are included.

13

Table B : Description

The effects of various accident characteristics on the risk of driver injury when involved in a two car injury accident are shown in Table B. The percentages are derived using a statistical modelling technique. The most important consequence of analysing the data in this way is that the estimates of injury risk are independent of each other. For example, the estimates of injury risk on different road types are the best available estimates of the specific effect of road type, after the influences of variations in the other effects listed have been removed. The risks shown in the table relate to the average specific effects of those factors in injury accidents. Further explanation and information on the analyses are given in Appendix 5.

Table A shows the percentage of car drivers injured when involved in an injury accident for individual models of car. The percentages are derived from statistical models similar to those used for Table B but extended to allow for the effect of model of car.

Table B : Commentary

The rates shown relate to the average specific effects of those factors in injury accidents, after correcting for the influences of variations in the other factors listed. For example, the risks of injury tabulated for different sizes of car are corrected to allow for differences in the age and sex of their drivers.

Of the factors considered, those having the most influence on the risk of death or serious injury when involved in an injury accident are the speed limit of the road, the first point of impact and driver age. The most severe accidents occur on 60 mph roads, where the risk of death or serious injury to the driver is 3 times higher than on a 20 or 30 mph road. The risk of death or serious injury is about one quarter lower on a 70 mph road than on a 60 mph road, which is perhaps a reflection of the improved segregation of traffic on multi-carriageway roads. A driver is about three times more likely to be killed or seriously injured in a frontal or side impact collision than when their car is hit from behind. However a rear impact is more likely to result in slight injuries; these are likely to be whiplash neck injuries associated with either poorly fitted or non-existent head restraints.

Age is not a large influence on the overall risk of injury when involved in an accident, although there is increased susceptibility to death or serious injury in the over 55 age group. Women are less likely to be killed when involved in an accident, which may indicate involvement at lower impact speeds. However they are about 40 per cent more likely to be injured when involved in a two car accident than men. This could be due to the different size of women, and the fact that women are more likely to sit closer to the steering wheel making them more prone to injury.

Table B Risk of injury to drivers involved in two car injury accidents: by various factors: 1989 to 1992

Percentage of drivers injured when involved in a two car injury accident[1]

| Factor | Injury severity[2] | | |
	Fatal	Fatal or Serious	All
Speed limit of road (mph)			
20 or 30	0.2	5	59
40 or 50	0.7	8	61
60	1.9	16	71
70	2.0	12	60
Sex of driver			
Male	0.5	7	54
Female	0.3	8	76
Age of driver			
17 - 24	0.4	7	63
25 - 34	0.3	7	61
35 - 54	0.4	7	62
55 or more	1.1	10	68
Size of car			
Small	0.6	9	72
Small/medium	0.4	8	63
Medium	0.4	7	57
Large	0.2	5	46
First point of impact			
Front	0.5	9	53
Back	0.1	3	83
Offside	0.9	10	71
Nearside	0.9	9	64
All accidents	0.4	8	63

1   Excluding accidents in which neither driver was injured.
2   Corrected for influences of variations in the other factors listed.

Summary

The risks of driver injury in injury accidents for particular popular models of car are presented as rates or proportions of driver injuries in Table A. The rates reflect the secondary protection offered to the driver, but also reflect the influence of mass in collisions. A problem in comparing rates, to assess the relative secondary safety of cars, is the influence of variability in accident severity. In each collision the relative severity of accident for each vehicle depends on the differences in mass between the vehicles, and also the type of accident and drivers involved. The variation in risk of driver injury due to the latter influences is accounted for by a modelling procedure which suggests that only minor adjustments should be made to the risks of driver injury in each model of car. The assumption that each model of car has a similar distribution of collisions in terms of the size of the other car involved implies that each car is effectively being assessed against a car of average mass. Any variation in driver injury risk due to differences in the size distribution of two car collisions is therefore likely to be minimal. The ratings in Table A retain the influence of mass, and support the indication that heavier cars tend to be safer cars for their occupants. However, within size groups where car mass is less variable, there are discernible differences in risk of driver injury.

It is also clear that heavier cars tend to increase the risk of injury in the cars they collide with, and the Department is assessing the possibility of producing indicators of relative aggressivity, both to other car drivers and other road users, for popular models of car, to supplement the measures of relative safety published in Table A and the Department's booklet on car safety and security.

The estimation of injury risk, and derivative car safety ratings, from road accident injury data is inevitably an evolutionary process. Methods of analysis are not static, and the amount of accident data available for a particular model of car gradually accumulates while a model is still active on the roads. Nevertheless the data records used to date do highlight some vehicles which are statistically better or worse than others, and provide some indication of relative safety. The data are recognised as a useful tool for informing car consumers about the safety features of cars, and for promoting the importance of car safety as a means of saving lives and avoiding serious injury.

PART 2

PRIMARY CAR SAFETY (Tables C and D)

Measuring Primary Car Safety

The risk of being involved in accidents is influenced mainly by driver behaviour, because the vast majority of accidents are initiated by driver error. However, vehicle characteristics such as braking, handling, lighting and drivers' fields of vision, known as primary safety factors, can influence the effects of driver error on accident risk, as can the road and traffic management infrastructure. In addition to these factors, the number of road injury accidents involving a particular type of vehicle will depend on the number of such vehicles on the road and the average mileage driven. These influences are known collectively as measures of exposure. Part 2 examines the involvement and casualty rates of different groups of car in injury accidents but the data do not fully account for exposure.

The Department obtains information on vehicle populations through analysis of Driver and Vehicle Licensing Agency (DVLA) registrations data. The stock figures used in these analyses are end of year figures, however this snapshot inherently overestimates the numbers of new cars and underestimates the number of old cars in relation to the average stock during the year. In order to provide a more balanced picture the stock figures incorporate factors aimed at giving a closer estimate of average stock. Further details of these adjustments can be found in Appendix 6.

The accident involvement and car user casualty rates in this section are given per 10,000 licensed vehicles in each group. General information on the drivers and average mileage covered by different types of car is available from the National Travel Survey and is summarised in Appendix 7. This shows that company cars record higher mileages than privately owned cars, and that newer cars record higher mileages than older cars.

The reliability of each accident involvement and casualty rate presented in Part 2 depends on the number of licensed cars in that category. For this reason, the rates are not quoted for car types with populations of less than 20,000 licensed vehicles.

Tables C : Description

Table C shows the extent to which drivers and their cars become involved in injury accidents. This is influenced mainly by driver behaviour, average mileage and pattern of use. The safety characteristics of the car will also have some influence but this is difficult to assess.

The table shows rates of involvement in injury accidents per 10,000 licensed vehicles in each of a number of groups. All injury accident involvements are included, regardless of whether the injured person was inside the car or not. Information is shown by size of car, private or company ownership, age of car, and by severity of injury.

The purpose is to illustrate differences in the rate of involvement in injury accidents for different groups of car. General information on car use, by age of car, engine capacity and ownership, extracted from the National Travel Survey, is summarised in Appendix 7.

Table C : Commentary

It is important to remember that differences in rates between groups in Table C will strongly reflect differences in the level and type of use and of driver behaviour, and should be interpreted carefully. The table shows the following:

- Drivers of new privately owned cars are involved in less accidents than drivers of new company owned cars. This may largely be explained by the National Travel Survey data which shows that in general company owned cars record higher mileages than privately owned cars.

- Drivers of high performance cars generally have higher rates of involvement in injury accidents than drivers of their standard performance counterparts.

- This distinction is much less clear for company owned cars where standard and high performance cars have very similar involvement rates.

- Newer private cars are seen to have lower rates of involvement in injury accidents than older cars, despite the evidence in Appendix 7 which shows that newer cars on average cover more miles each year.

Table D : Description

Table D shows car user casualty rates, which are influenced by the combined effects of accident involvement, accident type, the number of passengers and secondary safety features.

The table shows car user casualty rates per 10,000 licensed vehicles. Only persons injured while travelling inside the car are included in these rates. Information is shown by size of car, private or company ownership, and by severity of injury to occupant.

The average number of passengers carried has a much greater influence on the rates presented in Table D. However the accident reporting system does not require the police to record the number of uninjured passengers, so it is difficult to assess the size of this influence on the figures presented.

Table D : Commentary

Again, interpretation of the figures in this table depends on the relative mileages of the different types of car, their patterns of use and the behaviour of their drivers. The table shows the following:

- In most groups about 1 car user is killed and 10 to 12 seriously injured each year for every 10,000 licensed vehicles.

- The car user casualty rates show a tendency to decline with increasing size of car, although the relationship is less strong for fatal casualties.

- Among older cars, company owned vehicles have generally lower casualty rates than privately owned vehicles.

- Overall, newer private cars have lower casualty rates than older cars.

- High performance cars generally have higher casualty rates than their standard performance counterparts.

Table C Rates of involvement in injury accidents: by size of car and ownership: 1992

			Privately owned				Company owned	
			Injury accident severity				Injury accident severity	
		Fatal	Serious	All		Fatal	Serious	All
Regd. on or since 1.1.90								
Standard								
	Small	1.7	17	119		4.2	39	277
	Small/medium	1.8	17	112		3.8	37	244
	Medium	2.0	17	107		4.1	30	200
	Large	1.9	16	94		3.3	21	144
All standard		1.8	17	112		3.8	31	206
High								
	Small	3.3	30	170		3.7	39	238
	Small/medium	2.8	18	123		3.9	25	175
	Medium	3.1	16	114		4.2	26	161
All high		3.0	20	132		4.1	27	172
Registered before 1.1.90								
Standard								
	Small	1.9	22	145		2.0	26	163
	Small/medium	2.2	25	159		3.1	27	190
	Medium	2.3	26	160		2.5	28	179
	Large	2.3	21	129		1.9	18	116
All standard		2.2	24	152		2.4	25	162
High								
	Small	5.0	37	214		..	..	..
	Small/medium	3.9	33	196		2.2	30	174
	Medium	2.6	25	142		4.6	23	157
All high		3.7	31	183		3.7	26	166

Injury accident involvements per 10,000 licensed vehicles in each group

.. Denotes fewer than 20,000 licensed vehicles in the group.

Table D   Car user casualty rates: by size of car and ownership: 1992

		Car user casualties per 10,000 licensed vehicles in each group					
Age of car		Privately owned			Company owned		
Performance		Injury severity			Injury severity		
Size	Fatal	Serious	All	Fatal	Serious	All
Regd. on or since 1.1.90							
Standard							
Small	0.9	10	86	1.7	20	187
Small/medium	0.8	9	72	1.6	16	136
Medium	0.9	8	64	1.0	12	96
Large	0.5	6	46	0.8	5	56
All standard	0.8	9	73	1.1	12	106
High							
Small	1.1	16	112	2.2	27	167
Small/medium	1.5	10	72	2.7	12	87
Medium	1.9	7	64	1.1	9	74
All high	1.5	10	79	1.7	12	87
Registered before 1.1.90							
Standard							
Small	1.1	13	106	0.9	15	114
Small/medium	1.1	13	105	1.1	11	107
Medium	0.9	12	92	0.8	11	89
Large	0.7	8	61	0.4	5	45
All standard	1.0	12	97	0.8	10	84
High							
Small	2.8	25	158	..	..	..
Small/medium	1.8	18	128	1.5	14	104
Medium	1.2	12	81	1.8	11	72
All high	1.8	17	120	1.6	12	90

.. Denotes fewer than 20,000 licensed vehicles in the group.

APPENDIX 1   BACKGROUND AND DETAILED NOTES

Introduction

By agreement between the Department of Transport and police forces throughout Great Britain, details of all road accidents reported to the police in which a person is injured are transmitted to the Department of Transport in the form of a standard report (STATS19), usually through the appropriate local authority. These accident reports provide the basis for the Department's work on monitoring and analysis of road accident statistics.

From January 1989 the standard report prepared by the police was modified to include the registration marks of all motor vehicles involved in accidents. By linking the registration marks with the vehicle data held by DVLA at Swansea, a range of extra information about the vehicles involved in injury accidents can now be obtained. No personal details, such as names or addresses, are collected in this process.

This is the fourth report of results based on these additional vehicle data. It presents estimates of injury risk to drivers involved in injury accidents for popular car models, and also injury accident rates for different types of car and the types and numbers of casualties resulting from these accidents. The first report of this type, covering accidents in 1989, was published by HMSO in May 1991.

Coverage

It is not possible to link all vehicles involved in road injury accidents with vehicle registration data at DVLA. Details of foreign, diplomatic and military vehicles and those with trade plates are not held at DVLA. In addition, registration marks are generally unavailable for vehicles which leave the scene of an accident and some registration marks which appear to have a valid format prove untraceable.

In 1991 and 1992 these factors collectively resulted in roughly 16 per cent of vehicles having no additional vehicle details. Due to the varying rates at which registration marks began to be recorded by police forces the corresponding figure for 1989 and 1990 was higher than this.

The number of two car collisions analysed to produce the tables in Part 1 of this report is considerably lower than the number of two car collisions recorded in, say, the Department's annual publication Road Accidents Great Britain. This difference is due to several factors. Using the number of two car collisions shown in Table 23 of Road Accidents Great Britain (1989-92) as a base, the following table illustrates how this totality is reduced to the subset of collisions used in the analysis in Part 1 of this report, and the importance of each specific factor to the data reduction.

Table 23 (Road Accidents Great Britain 1989-92)	- 253714	(100%)
Exclusions due to vehicle registration data unavailable for both cars	- 177600	(70%)
Exclusions due to finer definition of car (based on detailed bodytype codes), involvement of parked cars or cars with no reference to impact with other car	- 134468	(53%)
Exclusion of accidents in which neither driver was injured	- 109135	(41%)

In order to be included in the analysis it is necessary to have the vehicle registration data of **both** cars involved. Although, for the reasons outlined in the preceding paragraphs, the detailed vehicle data is available for over 80 per cent of the cars, the requirement to have data for both cars results in approximately 70 per cent of the two car accidents (as published in Road Accidents Great Britain) being included in the analysis.

The number of accidents is further reduced due to several refinements to the dataset which aim to ensure that cars are being compared on as even a basis as possible. This involves narrowing the broader definition of car that is used for other publications and excluding accidents involving parked cars. In addition the analysis is restricted to accidents in which one or both of the drivers was injured. The resultant dataset, designed to minimise variation in accident types between different car models which could unduly bias comparisons of driver injury risk in particular car models, contains just over 40 per cent of the two car accidents published in Road Accidents Great Britain. Accident types that could otherwise bias ratings are therefore directly eliminated from the analysis. If they had been retained the relatively less powerful procedure of having to allow for their influence in a more complex modelling process would have had to be adopted.

Any bias due to missing data would be unlikely to significantly influence the ratings. It is reasonable to expect that missing data are unlikely to be concentrated in particular types of accidents for particular models of car, but are more likely to be randomly spread over all accident types and all models of car. Tests were conducted to check that the final dataset is typical of all two car collisions in terms of driver and accident characteristics. The results, shown below, demonstate that in terms of driver sex, driver age and speed limit of road the dataset used in the secondary safety analysis is representative.

Two car collisions by accident/driver type (%), 1989-92

	Road Accidents GB Table 23	Cars: Make and Model Table A
Speed limit of road		
20-39	61	58
40-59	11	12
60-69	23	24
70	5	5
Total	100	100
Driver sex		
Male	69	64
Female	31	36
Total	100	100
Driver age		
17-24	29	29
25-34	28	27
35-54	31	30
55+	13	13
Total	100	100

In previous years the risk of driver injury in different models of car was calculated using a broader definition of car accidents; this was found not to have significantly altered relative rankings of particular car models.

Other publications

Similar reports on car safety have been published in the United States of America by the Insurance Institute for Highway Safety, in Sweden by the Folksam Insurance Company, in Australia by the Monash University Accident Research Centre, in Finland by the University of Oulu and in the UK by the Transport Research Laboratory. Each produces a summary report for widespread distribution.

References:-

Insurance Institute for Highway Safety: Status Report. Vol 24, No 11.
1005 North Glebe Road, Arlington, VA 22201. ISSN 0018-988X.

Safe and Dangerous Cars 1989-90: A report from Folksam.
Folksam, Division for Research and Development, S-106 60 Stockholm.

The Effect of Driver's Age and Experience and Car Model on Accident Risk.
University of Oulu, Finland, Publications of Road and Transport Laboratory 1992.

Vehicle Crashworthiness Ratings: Victoria 1983-90 and NSW 1989-90 Crashes. Technical Report.
Monash University Accident Research Centre 1992.

The Theoretical Basis for Comparing the Accident Record of Car Models (Project Report 70).
Dr J Broughton, Safety Research Centre, Transport Research Laboratory 1994.

APPENDIX 2   DEFINITIONS

The statistics refer to accidents involving cars resulting in personal injury on public roads, including footways, which became known to the police. Results for 1992 include all accidents in that year determined by the date of accident. Tables in Part 1 also include data from 1989, 1990 and 1991 accidents. Figures for deaths refer to persons who sustained injuries causing death at the time of the accident or within 30 days of the accident, which is the internationally recognised definition.

Injury severity	*Severity* of an *injury* to a casualty is determined by the degree of injury and is either *fatal*, *seriously injured* or *slightly injured*.
Accident Severity	*Severity* of an *accident*, is determined by the severity of injury of the most severely injured casualty in that accident. That is *fatal*, where one or more persons involved in the accident were killed, *serious*, where one or more persons involved in the accident were seriously injured but no-one killed, or *slight*, where one or more persons involved in the accident were slightly injured but no-one killed or seriously injured.
Car	Any four-wheeled car. This includes saloons, hatch-backs, estates, "people carriers", coupes and convertibles. Purpose-built taxis, car derived vans, goods vehicles and minibuses are not included.
Size	Not formally defined but arranged so that the consumer can recognise standard groups. As an approximate guide, cars in the *small* group are generally between 140 and 150 inches in length and broadly equate to the motor industry's "minis" and "super-minis". Those in the *small/medium* group (equal to the industry's "lower medium") are between 155 and 165 inches, those in the *medium* group (= "upper medium") between 170 and 180 inches, and those in the *large* group (= "executive" and "luxury") over 180 inches.
	The allocation of a particular model to a size group does not imply that the model meets any formal classification or standard.
High performance	No single criterion has been adopted for the purpose of identifying cars in this category. Models whose performance is considerably higher than the standard production range are included. Most will be fitted with engines of higher capacity than their standard performance counterparts, and may also have features such as fuel injection or be fitted with turbo chargers. Typically, though not invariably, they have the capability of accelerating from 0 to 60 mph in 10 seconds or less.
	In the large group most cars are fitted with engines of greater power and higher cubic capacity. There is less distinction between standard and higher performance cars, so all cars in this size group have been classed as standard performance.
New and *Old* cars	Used in this report to describe cars registered on or after 1st January 1990 and before 1st January 1990 respectively. That is *new*, to describe cars up to three years old at the end of 1992, and *old*, to

describe cars three years old or more at the same date.

Ownership type — Identified from the registered keeper record at DVLA. *Company* cars are registered in the name of a company or partnership. *Private* cars are registered in the name of an individual.

APPENDIX 3   NUMBER OF INVOLVEMENTS BY MAKE/MODEL IN TABLE A

Car size/model	Registration dates	Involvements	Car size/model	Registration dates	Involvements
SMALL			**SMALL/MEDIUM**		
CITROEN 2CV/DYANE	Jan 83 - Jul 90	300	FIAT STRADA/REGATA	Jan 83 - Jun 88	500
CITROEN AX	Jun 87 - Dec 92	816	FIAT TIPO/TEMPRA	Jul 88 - Dec 92	310
CITROEN VISA	Jan 83 - Jul 88	288	FORD ESCORT/ORION	Jan 83 - Aug 90	18571
FIAT PANDA	Jan 83 - Dec 92	1120	FORD ESCORT/ORION	Sep 90 - Dec 92	1137
FIAT UNO	Jun 83 - Dec 92	2146	HONDA CIVIC	Oct 87 - Oct 91	239
FORD FIESTA	Jan 83 - Mar 89	9222	HYUNDAI PONY	Oct 85 - Aug 90	241
FORD FIESTA	Apr 89 - Dec 92	2767	LADA RIVA	Jan 83 - Dec 92	957
NISSAN MICRA	Jun 83 - Dec 92	2562	LADA SAMARA	Nov 87 - Dec 92	276
PEUGEOT 205	Oct 83 - Dec 92	3169	LANCIA DELTA/PRISMA	Jan 83 - Dec 92	150
RENAULT 5	Jan 83 - Jan 85	313	MAZDA 323	Jan 83 - Aug 85	197
RENAULT 5	Feb 85 - Dec 92	1581	MAZDA 323	Sep 85 - Sep 89	286
ROVER METRO	Jan 83 - Mar 90	7546	NISSAN CHERRY	Jan 83 - Aug 86	800
ROVER METRO	Apr 90 - Dec 92	528	NISSAN SUNNY	Jan 83 - Aug 86	1119
ROVER MINI	Jan 83 - Dec 92	1591	NISSAN SUNNY	Sep 86 - Jan 91	1259
TALBOT SAMBA	Jan 83 - Sep 86	393	PEUGEOT 305	Jan 83 - Jul 88	432
VAUXHALL NOVA	Apr 83 - Dec 92	4019	PEUGEOT 309	Feb 86 - Dec 92	1718
VOLKSWAGEN POLO	Jan 83 - Dec 92	1906	PROTON PROTON	Mar 89 - Dec 92	197
YUGO 3/4/500	Jan 83 - Dec 91	165	RENAULT 19	Feb 89 - Dec 92	407
YUGO TEMPO	May 83 - Dec 92	300	RENAULT 9/11	Jan 83 - Jan 89	1065
			ROVER 200	Jun 84 - Sep 89	2274
TOTAL[1]		59667	ROVER 200/400	Oct 89 - Dec 92	937
			ROVER MAESTRO	Mar 83 - Dec 92	3552
			SEAT IBIZA/MALAGA	Oct 85 - Dec 92	367
			SKODA ESTELLE	Jan 83 - Jul 90	581
			TALBOT HORIZON	Jan 83 - Dec 85	359
			TOYOTA COROLLA	Sep 83 - Aug 87	491
			TOYOTA COROLLA	Sep 87 - Jul 92	460
			TRIUMPH ACCLAIM	Jan 83 - May 84	372
MEDIUM			VAUXHALL ASTRA/BELMONT	Oct 84 - Sep 91	6479
AUDI 80/90	Jan 83 - Oct 86	576	VAUXHALL ASTRA	Oct 91 - Dec 92	187
AUDI 80/90	Nov 86 - Dec 92	322	VAUXHALL CHEVETTE	Jan 83 - Aug 84	203
AUSTIN AMBASSADOR	Jan 83 - Jan 84	152	VOLKSWAGEN GOLF/JETTA	Jan 83 - Feb 84	538
BMW 3 SERIES	Jan 83 - Mar 91	1601	VOLKSWAGEN GOLF/JETTA	Mar 84 - Dec 92	3128
CITROEN BX	Aug 83 - Dec 92	1914	VOLVO 300	Jan 83 - Dec 91	1850
FORD SIERRA/SAPPHIRE	Jan 83 - Dec 92	11797			
FSO POLONEZ	Jan 83 - Dec 91	156	TOTAL[1]		67652
HONDA ACCORD	Oct 85 - Sep 91	436			
HONDA PRELUDE	Mar 83 - Mar 92	173	**LARGE**		
HYUNDAI STELLAR	Jun 84 - Dec 92	219	AUDI 100/200	Jan 83 - Dec 92	348
MAZDA 626	May 83 - Sep 87	296	BMW 5 SERIES	Jan 83 - May 88	426
MAZDA 626	Oct 87 - Jan 92	214	BMW 5 SERIES	Jun 88 - Dec 92	296
MERCEDES 190	Sep 83 - Dec 92	428	FORD GRANADA	Jan 83 - Apr 85	534
NISSAN BLUEBIRD	Mar 86 - Aug 90	1907	FORD GRANADA	May 85 - Dec 92	1599
NISSAN STANZA	Jan 83 - Dec 86	334	JAGUAR XJ	Oct 86 - Dec 92	400
PEUGEOT 405	Jan 88 - Dec 92	1279	MERCEDES 200/300	Jan 83 - Sep 85	183
RENAULT 18	Jan 83 - May 86	249	MERCEDES 200/300	Oct 85 - Dec 92	369
RENAULT 21	Jun 86 - Dec 92	712	PEUGEOT 505	Jan 83 - Dec 91	246
ROVER MONTEGO	Apr 84 - Dec 92	3482	RENAULT 25	Jul 84 - Dec 92	460
SUBARU 1.6/1.8	Nov 84 - Dec 91	185	ROVER 800	Jul 86 - Dec 92	1026
TALBOT ALPINE/SOLARA	Jan 83 - Dec 86	355	ROVER SD1	Jan 83 - Jun 86	387
TOYOTA CAMRY	May 83 - Dec 86	222	SAAB 900	Jan 83 - Dec 92	377
TOYOTA CARINA	Apr 84 - Feb 88	263	SAAB 9000	Oct 85 - Dec 92	187
TOYOTA CARINA	Mar 88 - Apr 92	207	VAUXHALL CARLTON	Jan 83 - Oct 86	594
VAUXHALL CAVALIER	Jan 83 - Sep 88	5201	VAUXHALL CARLTON	Nov 86 - Dec 92	849
VAUXHALL CAVALIER	Oct 88 - Dec 92	3159	VAUXHALL SENATOR	Sep 87 - Dec 92	258
VOLKSWAGEN PASSAT/SANTANA	Jan 83 - May 88	393	VOLVO 200	Jan 83 - Dec 92	667
VOLKSWAGEN PASSAT	Jun 88 - Dec 92	230	VOLVO 700	Jan 83 - Jul 91	914
VOLVO 400	Jun 87 - Dec 92	325			
			TOTAL[1]		17951
TOTAL[1]		59894			

1 Totals include listed models, models whose sample size was insufficient and models whose first registration date is earlier than 1 January 1983.

APPENDIX 4   DISTRIBUTION OF INVOLVEMENTS BY SIZE OF COLLISION PARTNER (TABLE A)

Car size/model	Registration dates	Collision Partner Size Group (%)				
		Small	Small/ Medium	Medium	Large	Total
SMALL						
CITROEN 2CV/DYANE	Jan 83 - Jul 90	27	36	29	8	100
CITROEN AX	Jun 87 - Dec 92	28	34	32	7	100
CITROEN VISA	Jan 83 - Jul 88	26	34	29	11	100
FIAT PANDA	Jan 83 - Dec 92	29	35	29	6	100
FIAT UNO	Jun 83 - Dec 92	27	35	29	9	100
FORD FIESTA	Jan 83 - Mar 89	29	34	30	8	100
FORD FIESTA	Apr 89 - Dec 92	28	34	30	8	100
NISSAN MICRA	Jun 83 - Dec 92	30	32	30	9	100
PEUGEOT 205	Oct 83 - Dec 92	29	33	29	8	100
RENAULT 5	Jan 83 - Jan 85	31	34	25	11	100
RENAULT 5	Feb 85 - Dec 92	28	34	29	9	100
ROVER METRO	Jan 83 - Mar 90	28	34	30	8	100
ROVER METRO	Apr 90 - Dec 92	26	34	32	9	100
ROVER MINI	Jan 83 - Dec 92	26	35	31	9	100
TALBOT SAMBA	Jan 83 - Sep 86	31	31	31	7	100
VAUXHALL NOVA	Apr 83 - Dec 92	27	35	30	8	100
VOLKSWAGEN POLO	Jan 83 - Dec 92	29	31	31	8	100
YUGO 3/4/500	Jan 83 - Dec 91	33	31	28	8	100
YUGO TEMPO	May 83 - Dec 92	30	39	24	6	100
ALL SMALL		28	34	30	8	100
SMALL/MEDIUM						
FIAT STRADA/REGATA	Jan 83 - Jun 88	30	34	32	5	100
FIAT TIPO/TEMPRA	Jul 88 - Dec 92	26	35	32	7	100
FORD ESCORT/ORION	Jan 83 - Aug 90	29	35	29	7	100
FORD ESCORT/ORION	Sep 90 - Dec 92	31	33	30	6	100
HONDA CIVIC	Oct 87 - Oct 91	29	32	30	9	100
HYUNDAI PONY	Oct 85 - Aug 90	32	32	29	8	100
LADA RIVA	Jan 83 - Dec 92	31	32	29	8	100
LADA SAMARA	Nov 87 - Dec 92	33	34	25	7	100
LANCIA DELTA/PRISMA	Jan 83 - Dec 92	23	37	33	7	100
MAZDA 323	Jan 83 - Aug 85	29	35	27	9	100
MAZDA 323	Sep 85 - Sep 89	30	30	32	8	100
NISSAN CHERRY	Jan 83 - Aug 86	29	33	31	7	100
NISSAN SUNNY	Jan 83 - Aug 86	28	35	30	7	100
NISSAN SUNNY	Sep 86 - Jan 91	29	35	30	7	100
PEUGEOT 305	Jan 83 - Jul 88	31	29	31	10	100
PEUGEOT 309	Feb 86 - Dec 92	29	35	29	8	100
PROTON PROTON	Mar 89 - Dec 92	33	33	25	9	100
RENAULT 19	Feb 89 - Dec 92	30	34	28	7	100
RENAULT 9/11	Jan 83 - Jan 89	29	34	29	7	100
ROVER 200	Jun 84 - Sep 89	31	32	29	8	100
ROVER 200/400	Oct 89 - Dec 92	31	32	29	8	100
ROVER MAESTRO	Mar 83 - Dec 92	30	34	28	7	100
SEAT IBIZA/MALAGA	Oct 85 - Dec 92	29	36	28	7	100
SKODA ESTELLE	Jan 83 - Jul 90	30	32	32	6	100
TALBOT HORIZON	Jan 83 - Dec 85	28	33	30	9	100
TOYOTA COROLLA	Sep 83 - Aug 87	28	33	31	8	100
TOYOTA COROLLA	Sep 87 - Jul 92	29	37	30	4	100
TRIUMPH ACCLAIM	Jan 83 - May 84	32	28	33	7	100
VAUXHALL ASTRA/BELMONT	Oct 84 - Sep 91	30	34	28	7	100
VAUXHALL ASTRA	Oct 91 - Dec 92	34	27	31	8	100
VAUXHALL CHEVETTE	Jan 83 - Aug 84	31	33	27	8	100
VOLKSWAGEN GOLF/JETTA	Jan 83 - Feb 84	30	32	29	9	100
VOLKSWAGEN GOLF/JETTA	Mar 84 - Dec 92	31	33	28	9	100
VOLVO 300	Jan 83 - Dec 91	32	34	27	7	100
ALL SMALL/MEDIUM		30	34	29	7	100

Car size/model	Registration dates	Collision Partner Size Group (%)				
		Small	Small/ Medium	Medium	Large	Total
MEDIUM						
AUDI 80/90	Jan 83 - Oct 86	28	33	29	9	100
AUDI 80/90	Nov 86 - Dec 92	35	29	29	7	100
AUSTIN AMBASSADOR	Jan 83 - Jan 84	31	36	26	6	100
BMW 3 SERIES	Jan 83 - Mar 91	28	32	31	9	100
CITROEN BX	Aug 83 - Dec 92	31	35	27	7	100
FORD SIERRA/SAPPHIRE	Jan 83 - Dec 92	30	34	28	8	100
FSO POLONEZ	Jan 83 - Dec 91	31	32	27	10	100
HONDA ACCORD	Oct 85 - Sep 91	28	33	30	8	100
HONDA PRELUDE	Mar 83 - Mar 92	27	35	32	6	100
HYUNDAI STELLAR	Jun 84 - Dec 92	34	32	30	4	100
MAZDA 626	May 83 - Sep 87	32	34	26	7	100
MAZDA 626	Oct 87 - Jan 92	31	33	28	7	100
MERCEDES 190	Sep 83 - Dec 92	30	32	29	8	100
NISSAN BLUEBIRD	Mar 86 - Aug 90	29	34	30	7	100
NISSAN STANZA	Jan 83 - Dec 86	31	35	27	7	100
PEUGEOT 405	Jan 88 - Dec 92	30	35	27	8	100
RENAULT 18	Jan 83 - May 86	29	35	29	7	100
RENAULT 21	Jun 86 - Dec 92	32	30	29	9	100
ROVER MONTEGO	Apr 84 - Dec 92	30	35	28	7	100
SUBARU 1.6/1.8	Nov 84 - Dec 91	35	25	32	9	100
TALBOT ALPINE/SOLARA	Jan 83 - Dec 86	29	36	26	9	100
TOYOTA CAMRY	May 83 - Dec 86	28	35	30	7	100
TOYOTA CARINA	Apr 84 - Feb 88	31	36	26	7	100
TOYOTA CARINA	Mar 88 - Apr 92	33	37	22	8	100
VAUXHALL CAVALIER	Jan 83 - Sep 88	29	35	28	7	100
VAUXHALL CAVALIER	Oct 88 - Dec 92	48	58	46	12	100
VOLKSWAGEN PASSAT/SANTANA	Jan 83 - May 88	29	35	27	9	100
VOLKSWAGEN PASSAT	Jun 88 - Dec 92	38	28	26	8	100
VOLVO 400	Jun 87 - Dec 92	32	36	27	5	100
ALL MEDIUM		30	34	28	8	100
LARGE						
AUDI 100/200	Jan 83 - Dec 92	32	34	25	10	100
BMW 5 SERIES	Jan 83 - May 88	31	34	27	7	100
BMW 5 SERIES	Jun 88 - Dec 92	34	31	29	6	100
FORD GRANADA	Jan 83 - Apr 85	33	29	29	9	100
FORD GRANADA	May 85 - Dec 92	29	34	29	8	100
JAGUAR XJ	Oct 86 - Dec 92	30	33	30	7	100
MERCEDES 200/300	Jan 83 - Sep 85	29	31	29	11	100
MERCEDES 200/300	Oct 85 - Dec 92	34	35	25	6	100
PEUGEOT 505	Jan 83 - Dec 91	35	26	28	11	100
RENAULT 25	Jul 84 - Dec 92	33	31	29	7	100
ROVER 800	Jul 86 - Dec 92	33	31	29	6	100
ROVER SD1	Jan 83 - Jun 86	30	36	27	7	100
SAAB 900	Jan 83 - Dec 92	27	35	31	7	100
SAAB 9000	Oct 85 - Dec 92	26	37	30	7	100
VAUXHALL CARLTON	Jan 83 - Oct 86	28	36	27	9	100
VAUXHALL CARLTON	Nov 86 - Dec 92	31	36	27	7	100
VAUXHALL SENATOR	Sep 87 - Dec 92	30	36	29	5	100
VOLVO 200	Jan 83 - Dec 92	31	34	29	7	100
VOLVO 700	Jan 83 - Jul 91	33	30	29	8	100
ALL LARGE		31	33	28	7	100

APPENDIX 5   EXPLANATORY NOTES TO STATISTICAL MODELLING IN TABLES A AND B

The risk of injury to a driver involved in an accident clearly depends on a range of factors. Table B shows that the age and sex of driver, the speed of road and point of impact can all effect the risk of injury.

Valid comparisons of the inherent secondary safety records of different models of car are therefore complicated. Involvement in a high proportion of accidents with a low risk of driver injury will tend to produce a better apparent safety record whereas involvement in a high proportion of accidents with a high risk of driver injury will tend to produce a worse apparent safety record.

In order to isolate individual influences, statistical modelling has been used, which works by imagining that the risk of injury depends on a range of factors. The models look at the influences on the logarithm of the odds of injury, sometimes called the logit function, rather than directly at the influences on the proportion of accidents resulting in injury. This technique, known as logistic regression or logistic analysis, allows the influences on the risk of injury to be isolated and treated in an additive way. Unfortunately, the resulting factors are difficult to interpret by a non-specialist readership, so they have therefore been used to calculate corrected estimates of the percentage of drivers injured.

The statistical analyses used for Table B form the basis for the make/model comparisons in Table A. The largest influences on risk of injury to the driver in an accident identified from the statistical models used for Table B are also included in the statistical analyses comparing models of car used for Table A. The results are the best available estimates of the underlying secondary safety record, corrected for differences in key accident circumstances that influence the risk of injury to the driver.

The reliability of the result for a model of car in Table A depends on the number of recorded accident involvements of that model. Only those models exceeding the threshold of 150 involvements are included. In order to indicate the reliability of figures relating to individual models all estimates are accompanied by their associated 95 per cent confidence interval.

APPENDIX 5   EXPLANATORY NOTES TO STATISTICAL MODELLING (CONT.)

Statistical model used for each injury severity risk in Table A:

$$Y_{jklmn} = \mu + B_j + C_k + D_l + E_m + M_n + \epsilon_{jklmn},$$

where $Y_{jklmn} = \text{Log}_e [\, P_{jklmn}/(1-P_{jklmn})\,]$

and $P_{jklmn} = n_{jklmn}/N_{jklmn},$

where N_{jklmn} = Number of drivers in group $_{jklmn}$

and n_{jklmn} = Number of injured drivers in group $_{jklmn},$

and where the effects are represented by: -

μ	Overall mean,
B_j	Speed limit of road,
C_k	First point of impact,
D_l	Sex of driver,
E_m	Age group of driver,
M_n	Effect for model of car, and
ϵ	Error term.

Statistical model used for each injury severity risk in Table B:

$$Y_{ijklm} = \mu + A_i + B_j + C_k + D_l + E_m + \epsilon_{ijklm},$$

where the effects are represented as above and by: -

A_i	Size of car.

30

APPENDIX 6   ADJUSTMENTS TO 1992 STOCK FIGURES USED IN PART 2

The rates in tables C and D reflect an improvement to the calculation of stock levels. It is felt that the stock figures which act as the denominator in the calculations for involvement and casualty rates should be an average rather than an end of year figure. In the case of new cars (ie those registered from January 1990) using the end of 1992 stock figure would include all new registrations during that year, clearly constituting an overestimation of new cars relative to the average for the year.

There is a similar effect in the opposite direction for old cars (ie those registered before January 1990) due to scrappage. The transfer of cars between private and company ownership is an additional influence in the calculation of these factors, for example the transfer of older company cars to private ownership partly offsets the effect of scrappage on the figure for old private cars but accentuates the effect on the corresponding figure for company cars. The factors have been calculated using information from the Department's Annual Vehicle Census and Vehicle Information Database.

Estimated Average Stock (1992) as a proportion of end of year stock:

Registered on or since 1.1.90

Privately owned: 0.87

Company owned: 0.90

Registered before 1.1.90

Privately owned: 1.02

Company owned: 1.34

APPENDIX 7   INFORMATION ON AVERAGE MILEAGE DRAWN FROM THE NATIONAL TRAVEL SURVEY 1989-91

1. Estimated annual average mileage of four wheeled cars, by age and ownership of car, 1989-91

	Company	Private
Up to 1 year old	22600	10400
Over 1 and up to 2 years old	21500	10200
Over 2 and up to 3 years old	18200	9200
Over 3 years old	14500	8100
All ages	19900	8500

2. Estimated annual average mileage of four wheeled cars, by engine capacity of car, 1989-91

Up to 1000 cc	6800
1001 to 1300 cc	7900
1301 to 1400 cc	10000
1401 to 1800 cc	10600
1801 to 2000 cc	13100
2001 cc or more	11500
All capacities	9600

Printed in the United Kingdom for HMSO
Dd 298117 C8 5/94 3396 17434